50 W to Eat Your Honey

Healthy Honey Recipes
for Mastering the Art of Honeylingus

By Adrienne Hew, CN

The Nutrition Heretic

Edited by Kathryn Spence

Copyright © 2014 Savor the Journey, LLC

All rights reserved.

ISBN-13: 978-1500681159
ISBN-10: 1500681156

DEDICATION

To my husband, Joe, who knows how to treat his Honey right

DISCLAIMER

The content of this book is provided as information only and may not be construed as medical or health advice. No action or inaction should be taken solely on the basis of the information provided here. Please consult with a licensed health professional or doctor on any matter relating to your health and wellbeing.

The information and opinions expressed in this book are believed to be accurate and factual based upon the resources available to the authors at the time of writing. Readers who fail to consult with the appropriate health authorities assume the risk of any and all injuries.

The publisher is not responsible for errors or omissions.

Books in the Health AlternaTips Series

Drowning in 8 Glasses: 7 Myths about Water Revealed

Frenching Your Food: 7 Guilt-Free French Diet Tips to Slim Down, Look Younger and Live Longer without Calorie-Counting or Strenuous Exercise

Books in the Affordable Organics & GMO-Free Series

50 Ways to Eat Cock: Healthy Chicken Recipes with Balls!

50 Ways to Eat Your Honey:
Healthy Honey Recipes for Mastering the Art of Honeylingus

Good Times, Great Food: Fighting Childhood Obesity and Picky Eating One Celebration at a Time (coming 2014)

A SPECIAL GIFT FOR YOU!

Fifty Honey recipes not enough? I had to cut this book off at 50 recipes to keep it with the Affordable Organics & GMO-Free Series, but I have some special bonus recipes that I wanted to share with you. Now you can get your hands on these exclusive recipes just for purchasing this book.

The recipes in this gift are donated by some of my favorite honey producers and body care professionals. I'm sure you're going to love them. Go to http://honeyling.us/bonus to claim your free gift today!

Table of Contents

DEFLOWERING 1
   SWEET SEDUCTION 3
   UNLOCKING THE DOOR TO PASSION 5
   BEE HOLOCAUST 13
   HONEYLINGUS THEN AND NOW 18
   ABOUT THE RECIPES IN THIS BOOK 25
      FATS *26*
      WHOLE GRAINS *29*
      DAIRY *31*
      SALT *34*
      HONEY *35*

BEVERAGES 39
   SWEET N STICKY SMOOTHIE 41
   SWEET & SASSY EGGNOG 42
   VELVETY SPICED COCOA 43
   MULLED WINE 44
   HONEY-MINT LEMONADE 45

APPETIZERS & SNACKS 47
   HONEY WANNA PARTY WINGS 49
   FINGER-LICKIN' HONEY WIENERS 50
   TASTE OF HONEY PLATTER 51
   STICKY NUTS 52

SAUCES, SPREADS & DRESSINGS ... 53
SIZZLING CRANBERRY SAUCE ... 55
HONEY BEEBEEQ SAUCE ... 56
HONEY CASHEW BUTTER ... 57
HONEY MUSTARD DRESSING ... 58
UNDRESSED HONEY DRESSING ... 59
TAKE ME NOW TOPPING ... 60

SALADS ... 61
UNTOSSED SALAD ... 64

SOUP ... 67
WARM & FUZZY WINTER SOUP ... 69

VEGETABLES ... 71
GLOSSY FRENCH TICKLED CARROTS ... 73
TANGY CUCUMBERS ... 74
HONEY-DRIZZLED TOMATOES ... 75
HONEY-STROKED ROOT VEGETABLES ... 76

BREADS ... 77
CAPTIVATING CORNBREAD ... 79
BUZZY BANANA BREAD ... 80

SIDE DISHES ... 83
BEGUILING BAKED BEANS ... 85
OOEY GOOEY YAMS ... 87

ENTREES 89
- GLAZED HONEY CHOPS 91
- MARRY ME HONEY CHOPS 92
- GLISTENING BAKED HAM 93
- DRUNK & DRIPPING DUCK BREASTS 94
- SULTRY DUCK IN AN ORANGE DRESS 96
- SILKY ASIAN CHICKEN THIGHS 97
- MISO SALMON GLACÉ 98

DESSERTS 99
- LUSCIOUS HONEY-VANILLA ICE CREAM ... 101
- HONEY-KISSED DOUGHNUTS 102
- BEENY BROWNIES 104
- RICOTTA WITH HONEY DRIZZLES 105
- BLAZING APPLE DELIGHT 106
- WHIPPED CREAM OF THE GODS 107
- ALEX'S PEACHES ITALIANO 108
- HONEY BLUEBERRY CRUMBLE 109
- HONEY-POACHED PEARS 111
- BODACIOUS BAKLAVA 112

SWEET REMEDIES 115
- KRUPNIKAS 117
- NAUGHTY HOT TODDY 119
- SLIPPERY SORE THROAT SOOTHER 120
- HIGH ENERGY DRINK 121
- TITILLATING HONEY TURNIP 122
- SWEET & SPICY CURE-ALL 123
- BEE STING ALLERGY OBLITERATOR 124

BASICS **125**
   BAKING POWDER 127
   CRISPY NUTS 128

APPENDIX **129**
   MEASUREMENTS & EQUIVALENTS 131
   RESOURCES 132

   ABOUT THE AUTHOR 137

DEFLOWERING

SWEET SEDUCTION

I was introduced to Honey as a young child. She wasn't served regularly in our home, but she was always in the cupboard, waiting for the chance to make an appearance. Even though her appearances were brief and sporadic, I knew she was something special — something I longed for. The mere mention of Honey conjured up comforting and even romantic images. Where else do we find a substance used as a term of endearment, able to inspire philosophers and statesmen alike, and willing to lend her name to a post-wedding ritual reserved for newlyweds?

Like most modern people, I only had Honey when I was sick. Usually she was blended into a cup of hot tea as a healthy alternative to white sugar or mixed with fresh lemon juice to soothe a sore throat. Her use beyond that, however, was not common.

Why? I wondered. Why was I so attracted to Honey yet couldn't stand her taste outside of these two uses? Her flavor was too overpowering to enjoy in sweet or savory recipes that called for sugar. Even putting her in hot cocoa after a day of playing in the snow was not welcome. Perhaps the only other use that I eventually made peace with was to enjoy her ever-sosparingly and on very rare occasions on hot, buttered toast…. but that was pretty much it.

Honey was a temptress — a decidedly female tease that drew me in with her promises of sweet ecstasy, only to leave me feeling empty and disappointed both during and after the experience. She confused me about what it meant to be feminine and alluring, throwing me into the arms of more assertive, masculine flavors that knew how to deliver on their promises.

What particularly confused me was the fact that my parents had always revered Honey. To them, Honey was something completely different. She symbolized the comforting memories of an unspoiled childhood in a less damaged environment that was Jamaica in the 1940s and 50s. Honey was truly a treat that they got to enjoy without worry of damaging teeth like white sugar did. Yet she was also a remedy used to treat many ills.

I longed to know *that* Honey as a child, but like so many people, who have been deceived, I eventually decided that Honey was a waste of my time. I even turned my back on her, deciding that other than in the case of a sore throat, Honey had no role to play in my life.

UNLOCKING THE DOOR TO PASSION

It wasn't until some time after my 17th birthday that I finally met the real Honey for the first time. She was very different from the impostor I had known in earlier years. I didn't realize, however, just how special she was until I brought her home to meet my mother.

Some months earlier, I had started shopping in health food stores with a Swiss friend who was unable to eat most foods found in the average American supermarket. The unusual, then "earthy", packaging of everything in the store intrigued me. Each time, I would return to the store to try a "new" and interesting version of some food or cosmetic item with which I already had some familiarity — rice, pasta, milk, bread, vegetables, lotion, shampoo --- you get the picture.

I spent the first six months or so of my health food adventure walking past a huge plastic container with a spigot on it. It was obvious what was in there and *not* just because of the handmade label on the front. I could see her silky body through the plastic and her sticky residue on the plate below the spigot. It was *her* — Honey — there again to tempt me.

At first, I was skeptical. How many times would I allow myself to be seduced, then let down by this temptress? As a broke college student, I didn't have the disposable income to write off another failed fling.

Looking back, it's hard to recall the exact reason that I decided to give Honey another chance. Perhaps I felt a sore throat coming on that day. Or maybe I had just gotten paid and had some extra cash to spend on, what at the time, seemed to me an extravagant indulgence. Or maybe I saw my Swiss friend buy some. Whatever the reason, I chose this particular rainy day to buy a small container of Honey.

Honey and my other finds for the day made their way home on the long ride back to the Bronx. After walking another 15 minutes from the train station to the house, I set the brown paper bag on the kitchen counter.

As I took the items out of the bag, one-by-one, my mother walked over to see what craziness I was up to.

"What's this?" she said pointing to the mysterious container.

"Honey." I replied in a low voice.

"Can I try some?" she continued.

"Sure." I said, passing her a spoon.

She opened the container and gently dipped the spoon inside. Upon placing the spoon inside her mouth, her eyes opened wide. Then she smiled, "*This* is what Honey tasted like in Jamaica!" she said.

At first, I was amazed that for once, my mother didn't find something I brought back from the health food store to be completely weird or borderline revolting. Then it dawned on me that this is the Honey I had heard so much about and that I longed to know for so, so long!

I grabbed a clean spoon and proceeded to dip it into the container. I tasted the Honey. "Oh my gosh!" I thought. "This *is* good!"

This Honey wasn't bitter or off tasting like the conventional Honey I had come to know. She was sweet and delicate, as I always had wanted her to be. She was… perfect!

IS ALL HONEY THE SAME?

Conventional Honey, the kind most confirmed Honey haters are likely to know, rarely contains much real Honey at all. Besides being pasteurized through high heat processing to kill off all her goodness, she is often mixed with various forms of processed sugars, chemicals, and even high fructose corn syrup. No wonder it tastes so gross!

Real Honey — real *raw* Honey — is produced in a cozy, cooperative environment called a hive. The leader of the hive, as you may know, is the queen bee. Her job is to lay an average of 1,500 eggs per day. Taking care of the queen and her babies are her sisters — up to 60,000 of them — who go out and feed on the nectar of some 2,000 flowers each per day.

As they make the rounds from flower to flower, their fuzzy little bodies attract pollen from the flowers, depositing it on other flowers fertilizing the plant to make food that we can eventually eat. Without bees performing this important task, we wouldn't have most vegetables, fruits, herbs and nuts that make up our diets. We also wouldn't have the sweet-smelling flowers that cheer us up when we're feeling blue.

This nectar the bees collect is carried back to the hive and stored in wax cells where it is transformed into Honey to feed the hive over winter. The additional pollen, which they store in pollen baskets, is carried back to the hive to feed the developing larvae.

There is a third type of bee integral to the hive. Drone bees are the males; their sole purpose is to impregnate the queen. After copulation, they die.

The structure and function of a hive has been compared to that of a monastery. Sexual activity aside, it is a communal effort where all the members of the hive work diligently for the survival of the colony. There is no room for selfishness. The life of a bee is one of service to the community, perhaps a lesson we humans can learn, if we want to live in harmony.

Despite her exquisite flavor, it would be disingenuous to say that I have eaten Honey to the exclusion of all other sweeteners after that first taste. Honey at first glance appears not to have the right consistency or flavor for certain foods. This was, however, an early experience that connected me to old-world culinary delights that I thought only existed in fairy tales.

This is often the case with Honey. In her unadulterated state, she has a power that few other foods can boast. She opens up a new world for people, who misunderstood her and other health foods before. She confirms that good food is about community, enjoyment and pleasure, not about guilt, shame or superiority.

Over the years, I have brought many a friend, family member and client over to the "light side" of whole foods merely by making this initial shift. Soon, people find themselves interested in exploring a wide range of flavors and foods that they may have misunderstood. As Honey crowds out highly refined sugars and fake sweeteners, so butter replaces margarine and sparkling mineral water overshadows soda. Similar to a dirty window that finally meets a squeegee for the first time, the palate gradually clears and what was once an unclear path to nutrition suddenly allows the light of eating for satisfaction and joy to shine in.

Before you delve into buying your own Honey, there are a few things for you to consider. To get the best quality with all its life-affirming properties, experts generally recommend that you want to choose one that has been extracted at temperatures no higher than that of the hive. Other acceptable products will carry the claims *raw*, *uncooked*, or *unpasteurized*. Theoretically, these should be fine as well, but note that some producers will fudge terminology to suit their own harvesting practices. If in doubt, you can always ask. I have often found that whole food producers, including beekeepers, are more likely to defend flawed harvesting practices (possibly even insulting your intelligence) before lying to you.

One stumbling block that most people encounter when switching to real Honey, as well as other whole organic foods, is the price. While Honey appears to be more expensive at first glance, it is actually far more attainable than most people realize.

First, Honey is nearly twice as sweet as sugar. So when using it as a replacement, a cup of Honey will last you twice as long as the same amount of sugar. *Ka-ching!*

Next, there is the consideration that unlike processed sugars, raw Honey contains all of its naturally occurring vitamins, minerals and enzymes intact. This makes it more nutritive than most other sweeteners. It is a little known fact that highly refined sugars and juices are not only devoid of these nutrients, but they actually strip the body of important nutrient reserves such as calcium. Although possible, Honey is far less likely to cause such damage. Switching to raw Honey as part of a diet rich in a wide range of foods can boost immunity, leading to less illness, which means less days off from work or school, fewer doctor visits and fewer drugs to get you through your day. *Ka-ching!*

My third money-saving tip is to make an effort to displace other sweeteners in your diet. One fatal mistake that people make when buying whole foods for the first time is trying to add them on top of what they are already eating. This is clearly an additional expense, yet I see people do this all the time out of habit or perhaps a fear that they will be left without their favorite junk food on hand. So make a firm decision to crowd out impostor sweeteners with real, whole sweeteners like raw Honey. Your body and your pocketbook will thank you. *Ka-ching! Ka-ching!*

While Honey is certainly a step up from the majority of sweeteners, be careful not to turn it into a free-for-all. That is why my final, and least popular, recommendation for making Honey affordable is to explore *other* flavors. The world is becoming increasingly addicted to sweet flavors with America leading the way.

It is no secret that smoking is highly addictive and dulls our sense of taste. What most people don't realize is that eating too much sweetener does something very similar with one important difference – the more sugary flavors we eat, the more we require to taste anything.

Believe it or not, bitter, salty, sour and spicy can be a taste sensation in your mouth and eating them regularly will naturally reduce your desire to eat only sweetened foods. Foods with these other flavors support various organs in the body. Salt (in a natural form like Celtic sea salt), for example, benefits the stomach and kidneys. Bitter foods are great for the kidneys and urinary tract. Hot spices will benefit the intestines and lungs. And sour flavors will benefit the kidneys and adrenal glands.

Nearly everyone I know claims to believe in "everything in moderation", yet few actually *follow* this popular saying. Aim to be one of the few, who actually follow this advice and reap the rewards.

These are just a few of the benefits to incorporating other flavors into your diet and by reducing your reliance on the taste of all things sweet overall, your body will learn to gravitate towards them almost effortlessly and build up your health in the process. *Ka-ching! Ka-ching!Ka-ching! Ka-ching!*

BEE HOLOCAUST

No discussion about Honey would be complete without acknowledging the current threats to *Apis millifera* — the Honey bee. Bees have it tough. Not only are they responsible for pollinating up to 40% of our food supply, but they are also under attack by a variety of bacteria, fungi, viruses, and mites as well as human activity.

The more widely talked about causes of *dying* bees are the tracheal (also called *acarine*) and Varroa mites. Tracheal mites take up residence in the breathing tubes of the bees, while Varroa mites work through more vampire-like action by sucking on their blood and spreading from hive to hive until they kill the entire colony. Other pests that can weaken a hive include the small hive beetle, wax moth and *nosema apis*, a microsporidian that normally only appears to be a threat when bees are unable to leave the hive to eliminate waste.

Bacterial threats (such as American and European foulbrood), fungal diseases (chalkbrood and stonebrood) and viral infections (such as chronic or acute paralysis, Israeli paralysis, black queen cell and deformed wing virus) all have disturbing ways in which they can destroy a bee colony. The most disturbing and puzzling of them all, however, is what is called Colony

Collapse Disorder (CCD), which emerged as *the* major threat to Honey bees in the 21st century.

Beekeeper David Hackenberg is credited with raising awareness about the phenomenon of disappearing bees in the United States. Back in the Fall of 2006, he found over 90 percent of his 400 hives completely abandoned by his bees, perhaps with the exception of the queen and some of the larvae or younger bees. Why would a colony of bees that work solely for the survival of the hive leave the babies and the queen behind? Even the experts don't quite know because "bees just don't do that."

Honey bees are hardy creatures that have adapted to environmental changes such as extreme weather and varying altitudes for millennia. Disappearing bees, though, appear to be a sign of a deterioration in environmental *quality* — namely due to systemic pesticides (introduced to North American agriculture three years prior to the advent of CCD) and genetically modified crops as well as industrialized beekeeping practices such as artificial insemination of the queen and replacing their Honey within the hive with sugar water.

The crazy thing about CCD is that hardly any dead bees are found in or near the abandoned hives. There are virtually no clues left behind as to what is happening to these bees or where they are going. Some studies of abandoned hives suggest that infestations of some of the previously mentioned viruses are somehow contributing to their disappearance. The general consensus, however, is that the build up of chemicals mainly from pesticides and genetically engineered crops are weakening the bees' immune systems and disorienting them so much so that they cannot find their way back to the hive. It only takes 24 hours away from the hive for a bee to die. So in their state of confusion, that appears to be exactly what they do.

Another likely contributor to CCD is the rise of monocrops such as soy, corn and wheat, which are not pollinated by bees. Once upon a time, bees would be able to forage on flowers across vast areas of North America moving from one climate zone to another as the onset of cold weather dictated, but as the land was razed to plant heavily subsidized grain and legume crops with barely any flowering crops in between, bees became more dependent upon man to literally truck them across the continent in search of suitable crops to pollinate.

There are still many other theories about why bees suddenly vanish including the arrival of Africanized European bees (also known as killer bees) to the Americas. Although they are prolific Honey producers, killer bees are known to decimate the hives of more docile Honey bees. For most beekeepers, their mean disposition makes them risky to work with, but in South America and some parts of the United States, beekeepers are considering them a viable alternative to *Apis millifera* because of their high yield and resistance to the mites as well as other diseases plaguing other Honey bees.

No matter how you cut it, the bees are being threatened and if they don't survive, we don't survive. The world already saw this over 50 years ago in China in what is referred to as the Great Famine. China has never been clear about the exact causes of the famine, but the slaughter of bees is likely to have been a major contributor.

In 1957, Chairman Mao launched a massive campaign to kill the sparrows, which he blamed eating the grain intended for people. After hundreds of millions of sparrows were slaughtered, however, insects — especially locusts — began to take over and destroy crops. As it turns out, sparrows weren't eating so much grain as they were controlling the insect population.

Nonetheless, there was an insect problem to control and Mao (in his infinite wisdom) ordered a pesticide-spraying program. As you might imagine, these pesticides weren't selective and took the Honey bees down with all the other insects. The result was nearly four years of famine and an estimated 30 million citizens dying of starvation. Even today, there are dead zones across China where no Honeybees survive and plants must be hand-pollinated by humans.

I don't mean to be alarmist, but as most of us these days have so little contact with the origins of our food supply, I feel it is important that we realize there is more than "just Honey" at stake here. Awareness of this dilemma gives us the control to make wiser and more informed choices about where we choose to spend our money, as well as how to support Honey producers who are working to improve bee populations.

If you would like to learn more about CCD and the plight of the bees, please refer to the "resources" section of this book for the titles of several Honey associations and films documenting the disappearance of bees.

HONEYLINGUS THEN AND NOW

In September of 2000, I was fortunate enough to travel back in time — circa 700 B.C. — to the funerary feast of the legendary King Midas. The feast, served at the Museum of Archaeology at the University of Pennsylvania, replicated the archaeological discovery of the king's tomb in 1957. An analysis of the food remnants left in the earthenware at the excavation site at Gordion in Central Turkey revealed many of the foods served at Midas's funeral — lentils, lamb, fennel, bread, figs, and a wine and beer beverage blended with mead (a.k.a. fermented honey).

Dogfish Head Brewery in Delaware was given the honor of recreating the beverage for the meal. The meal was exquisite, but *King Midas Golden Elixir* was definitely the hit of the evening. You can still buy it today, so look for it, if you have the chance.

While Honey was clearly appreciated in King Midas's time, don't think that our love affair with Honey began there. Although the earliest bee fossils on record date back to about 150 million years ago, one of the earliest depictions of Honey harvesting was carved inside a cave in Valencia, Spain around 7,000 B.C. An Egyptian carving from 3,000 years later shows more or less the same thing. While they were hunting down hives with the express purpose of scavenging their Honey, it is the Chinese who are credited with actively keeping beehives — a practice that would eventually catch on worldwide.

It didn't take long for Honey to be accepted as a source of comfort and good fortune to humans. The nymph, Melissa, in Greek mythology is credited with discovering and teaching the use of Honey. She is said to have nursed the god, Zeus, with Honey instead of milk and it is from her name that the Greek word for Honey (*Meli*) is derived. In ancient Rome, you would have been more likely to hear someone utter the words "May honey drip on you!" than "Good luck!" The Greek philosopher Aristotle called her "nectar of the gods". And the pharaoh, Cleopatra, is well known for taking baths in milk laced with Honey.

The fascination with Honey does not stop with pagan history though. Religious texts also reference Honey in many places. In the Bible, the land of Israel is referred to as "the land flowing with milk and honey". The book of Proverbs proclaims that "Gracious words are a honeycomb, sweet to the soul and healing to the bones." In the book of Isaiah, it is prophesied that the Messiah "will eat butter and honey that he may refuse the evil and choose the good."

Still there are more references to Honey in many other world religions. The Prophet Mohammed recognized Honey as a "remedy for every illness", recommending both Honey and the Koran as remedies for illnesses of the body and mind. A bowstring made of

Honey bees was on the bow used by Kamadeva, the Hindu god of love. And during the festival of Madhu Purnima, Buddhists give Honey to monks to commemorate a monkey's gift to the Buddha while he was staying in the jungle. The ancient Egyptians even used Honey to embalm the dead and as an offering to their gods.

In the Omo Valley of modern day Ethiopia, there is even a tribe where the men primarily eat Honey as their main food! But I wouldn't attempt to follow their lead. Many of these men are so fat that they look like pregnant women.

No matter where you look, it would appear that Honey affirms that good does indeed exist in the world. She is a symbol of hope, comfort, love, caring and the divine.

As alluded to in many of the references above, Honey has not only been adored for her sweet taste, but for her role in maintaining health and beauty as well. The often empty promises of over-the-counter drugs and fancy body care products has led many people to rediscover how powerful Honey can be in treating routine health concerns and skin care. With the resurgence of raw Honey as a preferable sweetener to processed sugar cane and fruit juices, however, consumers are rediscovering the many benefits to keeping a jar of raw Honey around.

As with other nutritive sweeteners, raw Honey is comprised of the sugars glucose and fructose, and contains only small amounts of vitamins and minerals. That is why many people believe that her true value lies primarily in her pollen, royal jelly, propolis and naturally occurring enzymes.

Today, most people only know Honey as a cure for sore throats, but since Roman times, she has been used to heal battle wounds of soldiers. She is also valued in many cultures as an ointment for burns and rashes.

Talk to people who have replaced pasteurized honey, refined sugars, juices and artificial sweeteners with raw Honey, and you'll find reports of Honey curing everything from lethargy and athlete's foot to arthritis and ulcers. The medical establishment would call these reports anecdotal and it's always important to know exactly *how* the Honey was used along with other changes in habits or diet, but doesn't it seem like a deliciously simple way to get relief from what ails you before jumping into taking dangerous drugs with bad side effects?

Studies have shown that eating Honey can reduce systemic inflammation by lowering homocysteine levels. As high levels of homocysteine are considered a risk factor for cardiovascular disease and renal dysfunction, it would appear that a little raw Honey would protect your heart and kidneys too.

Not everyone can eat Honey, though. It is widely discouraged to give to babies of less than one year for fear of botulism due to their immature digestive systems. For others, however, so long as a sugar-sensitive condition like diabetes is not present (although some diabetics report otherwise), Honey should be perfectly fine.

Suffice it to say that raw Honey is clearly far less injurious to health than refined sugars and artificial sweeteners. Should you choose to use Honey therapeutically and not just as a sweetener, be sure to get the input of a qualified practitioner as to the proper procedure to follow.

Even if for some reason you are unable to eat your Honey, you may still be able to use her topically. From skin irritations to anti-aging treatments, generations of women have sworn by the topical use of Honey.

When I suffered from extremely uncomfortable, bleeding eczema, putting diluted Honey on my skin for several minutes followed by a cool water rinse provided temporary relief that even the most expensive prescription creams couldn't offer. The topical use of Honey has also been noted to reduce wrinkles, scarring, acne, sunburns, cataracts and diabetic skin ulcers.

One form of Honey that has been getting a lot of attention in recent years is Manuka Honey from New Zealand and Australia. This Honey comes from bees foraging on flowers of the uncultivated Manuka tree. She is said to have higher potency and resilience than standard Honey, which is more prone to degrade when exposed to heat and light. Uses for Manuka Honey are the same as those for standard Honey, but she is generally regarded as more efficacious in her action.

    Personally, I have not had any particular successes during my trials of Manuka Honey even though I tested a few reputable brands. Manuka is rated in terms of her non-peroxide antimicrobial activity (called Unique Manuka Factor or UMF). The higher the number, the stronger this activity. If you decide to invest in Manuka Honey, however, be prepared to spend around US$20 for a 4-ounce jar of UMF 12+, more than double for UMF 20+. It is also worth noting that some Honey labeled Manuka may say 12+, for example, but will not say UMF or MGO (another acceptable certification). These are considered counterfeit, as they have not passed by the necessary certifying body.

    As previously mentioned, the gifts bees provide us with don't end with Honey.

- Beeswax is not only a component of many skincare products and candles, but also can be used to polish furniture, lubricate mechanical joints and in waterproofing leather.

- Bee pollen, which is said to contain up to 35% protein, is used in many cultures as medicine, namely for boosting immunity and eliminating allergies, but also has many other uses.

- Royal jelly, the milky substance used to nourish queen bees, is also used for eliminating allergies such as hay fever, skin conditions and asthma. It is perhaps best known, however, for its role in slowing the aging process.

- Propolis, a resin from poplar and cone-bearing trees, is usually obtained from beehives. Its antifungal, antiviral and antibacterial properties have been prized for millennia. It is typically used for healing wounds, as well as bacteria-related infections.

If you decide to use any of these products for serious health problems, please do your due diligence and get the help of a qualified practitioner. Although bee pollen, for example, has been used in the treatment of allergies, it is possible to have a severe allergic reaction to the pollen itself. Bee product reactions can be fierce, so don't mess around.

ABOUT THE RECIPES IN THIS BOOK

Although, you may find the title of this book funny, racy, or even raunchy, the information contained in these pages is written from my perspective as a nutritionist. If you are interested in dispelling some of the nutritional taboos that plague the way most people eat today, then read this section. If you just want to get started on eating your Honey, feel free to skip ahead to the recipes.

Fifty Ways to Eat Your Honey is part of my Affordable Organics and GMO-Free series of books. For many readers, it serves as an introduction to cooking traditional foods as well as a few preparation techniques that will increase the body's ability to use the nutrients contained in the foods you eat. For those already familiar with these techniques, it will hopefully serve as an additional resource for cooking delicious traditional foods that appeal to a modern palate.

That said, I am not your typical whole-foods nutritionist, hence the moniker, *The Nutrition Heretic*. Over the years, I have had many mentors including doctors, nutritionists and researchers. They have helped me understand that eating well can be simple, just by combining a diet of foods from both the plant and animal kingdom. Yet there are several key areas of nutrition where many conventional and holistic health practitioners continue to parrot semi-truths established by the food processing industry. These companies have made billions of dollars by scaring people away from real foods and then selling products that swoop in to save the day. Below are a few examples as they pertain to this book:

FATS

You will notice that many of the recipes in this book call for animal fats that nearly every other health professional in the United States would warn you *against* eating. Animal fats were a significant source of energy until 100 years ago. Contrary to popular belief, people who ate these fats routinely lived longer than people do today. In the book *Diet & Heart Disease*, author Stephen Byrnes notes that a report in the *Journal of American Oil Chemists* showed that "animal fat consumption had declined from 104 grams per person per day in 1909, to 97 grams per day in 1972, while vegetable fat intake had increased from a low 21 grams to almost 60 grams. Total fat consumption had increased, as the proponents of the Lipid Hypothesis argued, but this increase was mostly due to vegetable oils with 50 percent coming from liquid oils and the other 41 percent from margarine made from vegetable oils."

Comparatively, animal fats contain higher amounts of saturated fatty acids than modern vegetable oils. These fatty acids are easily recognized by the body and contribute to the body's healthy absorption of nutrients. The fact that saturated fat is an important nutrient for both the heart and intestines was once common knowledge published in nutrition and medical textbooks. This would conflict with modern nutritional dogma that wants us to believe that natural animal fats, the saturated ones in particular, are the cause of disease. The modern approach would have us believe that our bodies prefer to use fake, rancid oils and fats, such as margarine and canola.

In addition to their importance to the heart and intestines, animal fats are an important source of the fat-soluble vitamins A, D, E and K. They are also important to cellular integrity. Without saturated fats to lubricate the joints, mucous membranes and skin, joint disease, asthma and skin eruptions become common problems. Along with cholesterol, these fats regulate our hormones, prevent mood swings and slow the uptake of sugar in the blood.

Popular reports denigrating the use of saturated fats mistakenly describe them (and their cousin, cholesterol) as artery-clogging. Perhaps this would be true if they were hydrogenated, but just like all other natural foods, saturated fats break down into their original components (mainly smaller fatty acids and glycerol). In my opinion, a better way of looking at saturated fats is as antioxidants because they are very stable fats, which prevent the oxidation of unsaturated fatty acids, fats that are highly prone to rancidity.

Over the years, I have seen many clients, family, and friends lose weight or overcome conditions such as acne, constipation, joint degeneration, depression and infertility simply by exchanging soybean, canola, corn and other highly processed vegetable oils for schmaltz (chicken fat), lard, butter and even coconut oil (a saturated fat not derived from animals). Despite the list of benefits to eating saturated fats, drug and food processing companies have made trillions of dollars over the years by convincing us these fats cause disease.

When you make the switch to natural saturated fats, seek out *unhydrogenated* versions. If in doubt because of incomplete labeling, you will recognize unhydrogenated fats because they are soft or even semi-liquid at room temperature. Hydrogenated fats remain hard even at temperatures up to approximately 145°F. Fats from animals raised on pasture instead of feedlots is best, but as of the writing of this book, I consider *any* unhydrogenated animal fat to be better than any of the cheap vegetable oils that line supermarket and health food store shelves.

Two popular unsaturated oils that are fine to eat are extra virgin olive oil and sesame oil. Along with a few others, these plant oils have stood the test of time, however, that does not mean that fat consumption should be limited to these. Each oil or fat has different health benefits and temperature thresholds before they produce free radicals, volatile compounds, which have a high correlation with soaring cancer rates. So consuming a combination of fats and oils is wise.

As you can imagine, there is a wealth of information and misinformation about fat and cholesterol that are beyond the scope of this book. My intention here is to give you an overview of the reasons natural fats have been included in this book.

WHOLE GRAINS

Unlike some whole foods nutritionists, I am not hung up on using whole grains 100% of the time. In the current push to eat more fiber, few people are aware of the fact that massive amounts of fiber can irritate the delicate hair-like projections in the intestines called *villi* and even lead to constipation over time.

Nutrition researchers such as Sally Fallon Morell and Ann Wigmore have touted the importance of soaking or souring grains in an acidic medium (such as water with a touch of yogurt or lemon juice added) before cooking and eating them. Soaking helps to predigest grains and make all of their nutrients more bioavailable. This practice also breaks down the phytic acid in grains, which blocks nutrient absorption, and takes the harsh edge off of fiber, giving whole grain products a better mouth feel and easier transit through the digestive tract.

In my own experience, I have found that people who have suspected that they had gluten intolerance (a mechanical inability to digest the protein gluten in wheat and related grains) have suddenly discovered an ability to digest wheat and other gluten-containing grains properly as long as they are soaked in this manner. I have also noticed that nearly 100% of the people who have reported to me that they suffer from gluten intolerance have spent several months or years eating low-fat diets, high fiber, and/or whole grain foods that have *not* been prepared by soaking or fermenting. I believe that it is only a matter of time before a study is performed that proves that depriving the intestines of their preferred food (saturated fat) and the overconsumption of fiber are risk factors for gluten intolerance and even celiac disease (a genetic form of gluten intolerance, which involves a more biochemical reaction to the consumption of gluten-containing grains).

Properly preparing grains does not only apply to wheat, spelt, barley and other gluten-containing grains. It is a good practice for nearly every grain.

On the other hand, brown rice is one grain that does not require soaking prior to cooking. I do, however, find that it has a much more pleasant texture and flavor when soaked in filtered water with a splash of raw apple cider vinegar added to the soaking water.

So when it comes to grains, if you cannot prepare your whole grains properly by soaking them beforehand, I recommend choosing the least processed version you can find. For example, when choosing pasta, the ones I look to first are those made from brown rice, buckwheat or unenriched durum semolina. If you only eat pasta once or twice per month, this is an acceptable compromise food. Anyone truly suffering from either gluten intolerance or celiac disease would benefit from avoiding semolina, which is a form of wheat.

For pie crusts, I use unbleached, unenriched, and unbromated, preferably organic flour. Bleaching, bromating and enriching flour adds many undesirable contaminants to your foods including a host of heavy metals and chemicals.

DAIRY

Dairy has gotten a bad rap over the past few decades. First we were told that it was contributing to excessive weight gain, so we were convinced to consume only low or no fat versions of it. Now it seems that half the population believes that milk is incompatible with human physiology, despite the fact that we are mammals. So they begin drinking fake, highly processed "milks" made from soy, hemp, almonds and rice.

Few have contemplated the fact that our ancestors have consumed milk in one form or another since our early existence. Today, many societies still attribute their longevity to the consumption of dairy products. And while most everybody acknowledges that the French are skinnier and tend to live longer than Americans (despite eating plenty of butter and cream sauces), we still choose a tasteless, low-fat lifestyle.

Others argue that humans are the only mammals that drink milk of another animal past infancy. This popular myth runs rampant among city folk. We are also the only animals that cultivate crops, wear clothing, harness electricity, and watch reruns of "Seinfeld". So what? We drink other animals' milk because we can and it's good for us. Talk to any dairy farmer and they will tell you that many farm animals crowd around the milking room at milking time to lap up any milk that may spill outside of the room. It's good stuff!

The sad fact is that in the U.S. and increasingly around the world, milk is no longer a whole food. Like most vegetable oils, the milk that lines supermarket shelves is a rancid product that has been treated so as to not reveal its true age. Milk that has been pasteurized is defenseless against pathogenic bacteria such as listeria and *E. coli*. The largest salmonellosis outbreak in U.S. history affected nearly 200,000 people came from *pasteurized* milk produced at one dairy in Illinois. These pasteurized milk outbreaks occur relatively frequently and often involve the death of several people affected.

Homogenized milk is very difficult to digest because the fat molecules in the milk are pushed through screens at high pressures to artificially suspend them in the rest of the milk. As a result, the body has difficulty making sense of these kind of milk molecules when they enter the blood stream and over time may perceive it as a threat. This is likely to be one source of dairy allergies.

Alternatively, if you follow the advice to drink skim milk, you are merely drinking the lactose portion of the milk that has been tampered with. In light of the fact that lactose intolerance seems to be on the rise, I believe it would make more sense to drink the cream and toss the watery blue lactose portion of the milk instead.

On the other hand, *unpasteurized* milk is the way that our ancestors drank milk until a little over 100 years ago. Studies have shown that because it has not had its defenses (enzymes) killed off by the pasteurization process, raw milk can actually kill bacteria on contact. And that cream that I told you to drink in place of the skim portion of the milk? Yep, you guessed it. It can be a source of valuable fat-soluble vitamins and minerals that are very important to the health of your intestinal tract.

Just like with the animal fats from meats, if you are drinking raw milk, the best bet is to get it from pastured animals. Many states allow you to purchase directly from the farm often by belonging to a cow (or goat) share program, where you pay to be part owner of the animal and receive the benefits of what the animal produces. In a few states, you can even purchase this milk in stores. Check realmilk.org to find raw milk in your area.

SALT

Salt is essential to life. It stimulates the appetite as much as it satisfies the appetite. Salt helps you to digest your food, so it is important to add enough salt to your recipes so that they satisfy your taste buds.

That said, it is important to use real salt. I define real salt as any naturally occurring salt that is naturally dehydrated. The two basic types are Himalayan salt, which is mined, and naturally dehydrated sea salt from the ocean. Both contain moisture (sea salt more so than mined salt) so it is not uncommon for them to clump slightly in their packaging. They both also contain a wide array of minerals, including the often difficult-to-obtain trace minerals.

On the other hand, regular table salt is a highly refined substance. It contains mainly one compound — sodium chloride — along with a bunch of fillers. Unlike natural salts, table salt wreaks havoc on health and is associated with raising blood pressure. In cases where iodine is added to it, the iodine comes in a toxic form that is even more health damaging. Some people mistakenly believe Kosher salt to be a natural salt, but in fact, it is even more highly processed than regular table salt and should be avoided. Coarse sea salt is a much safer alternative to Kosher salt.

Conventional health practitioners make no distinction between the many types of salt on the market, and offer only blanket recommendations to avoid or limit salt. This has left many people not only with impaired digestion, but it also leaves food less satisfying. The result of the latter is overeating naturally low sodium foods, namely desserts.

Progressive health practitioners, however, will encourage their patients to consume naturally dried sea salt or Himalayan salt on their food, and even in their water. In fact, many have found that unlike regular salt, these natural salts help *lower* blood pressure and improve poor digestion.

Recommendations for my favorite brands of salt and other quality ingredients may be found at the Nutrition Heretic product page.

HONEY

Last, but not least, there is Honey — the star of this book. While raw Honey is definitely the best, not all of the recipes use her in this pure form. In some cases, it is for texture. In other cases, it is because it would be impossible to add at the end (see the Desserts section).

While I feel it is important to take food quality and nutrient-retention seriously, I also feel it is important to keep eating a joyful experience. Many people fall off the wagon of eating whole foods because they obsess over little details. I would rather make small compromises in areas I can control rather than to go hog wild on something really damaging (that probably won't even taste as good) when I leave the house. For me, a Honey-Kissed Doughnut will always win over a Dunkin' Donut. My kids agree.

Susan Ledbetter, who runs the popular *Honey Bee Kind* workshops in Alabama, has some tips for people who want to replace the sugar in their recipes for baked goods with Honey:

- For every cup of Honey, you will need to reduce other liquids by ¼ cup
- Add a ½ tsp baking soda for every cup on Honey used
- Reduce oven temperature by 25°F to prevent burning of sugars in Honey

Considering the above, note that should you choose to replace any of my ingredient recommendations with conventional ones, substitute granular sugar for Honey or ignore the grain preparation techniques in this book, keep in mind that you may need to adjust liquid requirements and cooking times. With all this in mind, let's get cooking!

11 Things You Can Do to Help Save the Bees

- Eat a wide range of food, including meats, fish, eggs, dairy, vegetables, nuts, legumes, fruits and starches, to reduce the burden on the bees.

- Plant flowers, or grow fruits and vegetables.

- Buy Honey from your local beekeeper. Check out smaller health food stores and farmer's markets.

- Go organic and biodynamic! Avoid GMOs and foods grown with pesticides as much as possible.

- Avoid foods containing canola oil, which comes from a genetically engineered rapeseed, whether or not it is "organic".

- If you eat grains, try to avoid conventionally produced ones raised on commercial farms. Some small farms and co-ops are beginning to raise their own grain and sell the flour. Seek them out.
  Consume fewer monocrops – especially wheat, corn and soy – because they are sprayed with the harmful pesticides that lead to CCD.

  Become a beekeeper. Even New York City allows rooftop beekeeping, so don't fret if you live in an apartment in the city. Contact your local beekeeping association for information on classes.
- Adopt a swarm. Your local beekeeping association will know about this too.

- Get involved. Demonstrate, sign petitions, make a donation, vote, or talk to friends and neighbors. Any act, big or small, to raise awareness will make a difference!

- Give a copy of this book to your friends and family! A percentage of profits from the sale of this book goes to save the bees.

BEVERAGES

SWEET N STICKY SMOOTHIE

Serves 4

Smoothies are a natural place to use honey. I make this fast and nutritious breakfast option in a quart-sized mason jar using a stick blender. Makes clean up a snap and storage is easy, if for some reason, there are any leftovers.

Ingredients:

    1 slightly overripe small banana

    5 fresh or frozen whole strawberries or equivalent of other berries

    3 cups whole milk yogurt or kefir

    2 tbsp flax seed oil (optional)

    1 tbsp raw honey

Place all ingredients in blender (or quart-sized jar or measuring cup). Blend on high speed for 15 seconds. Enjoy as part of a healthy breakfast.

SWEET & SASSY EGGNOG

Makes 6 generous servings

Here's a non-traditional spin on eggnog that tastes more like a shake than the sickeningly sweet concoction that lines supermarket shelves. If you're nervous about eating raw eggs, you won't need to be, as long as you buy good quality eggs direct from a reputable farmer.

Ingredients:

   3 cups heavy cream, preferably raw

   1 1/2 cups milk, preferably raw

   6 large egg yolks

   1/2 cup raw honey

   2 bottles Guinness extra stout or chocolate stout

   Freshly grated nutmeg

Place cream in the large bowl of an electric mixer and whip until frothy. Be careful not to whip into butter. If you tip the bowl and the cream doesn't budge, you've whipped it enough. Gradually add milk while continuing to whip. Drop eggs in, one at a time, then the honey with mixer still going. Finally, add the stout slowly to the mixture. Pour into glasses with a fresh grating of nutmeg on top for garnish.

VELVETY SPICED COCOA

Serves 4

While yummy, this may not seem like a very adventurous recipe. But preparing with a Jamaican-style kick will elevate it up another notch. If you really want to go all Jamaican, I suggest you buy Jamaican cocoa that has been pressed into huge balls. They are available at West Indian grocery stores. Simply grate the balls to obtain a powder that will semi-dissolve in the milk.

Ingredients:

1/4 cup powdered, unsweetened cocoa

1/4 cup filtered water

4 cups milk, preferably raw, but never ultra-pasteurized

1 4" cinnamon stick or 4 cinnamon leaves (available at West Indian grocers)

4 tbsp raw honey

In a medium sized pot, mix water and cocoa. Bring to a boil, then stir to blend well. Add milk and cinnamon. Heat gently to warm milk just above body temperature -- any higher and you will destroy all the enzymes in your milk. Remove from heat and add honey. Serve warm.

MULLED WINE

Serves 6

A nice alternative to the hot toddy, mulled wine

Ingredients:

> 1 bottle of red wine such as merlot, zinfandel, cabernet sauvignon or burgundy
>
> 1 inch slice of fresh ginger
>
> Juice and zest of an organic orange — zest should be peeled, not grated
>
> 3 4-inch cinnamon sticks
>
> 8 whole allspice berries
>
> 1/4 cup raw honey

Combine all ingredients in a large pot. Bring to a low simmer for 10 minutes. Serve warm in mugs with cinnamon sticks for stirring.

HONEY-MINT LEMONADE

Makes 2 quarts

Conventional honey makes lemonade taste awful. Here, it is paired with fresh peppermint for a refreshing twist on a hot and humid day.

Ingredients:

    Juice of 3 whole lemons (more, if not juicy enough)

    4 tbsp raw honey

    One small bunch of fresh peppermint

    Pinch of Celtic sea salt

    2 quarts filtered water

In a glass pitcher, place mint, sea salt and half of the honey. Crush peppermint leaves with the end of a wooden rolling pin or spoon to release the mint oils. Add water, lemon juice and rest of honey. Blend well. Adjust for right amount of sweet and sour balance. Serve chilled.

APPETIZERS & SNACKS

HONEY WANNA PARTY WINGS

Serves 4 to 6

Wings are the hit of any party. Just make sure to place a clearly marked plate or bowl out for the discarded bones. Otherwise, your party can turn nasty fairly quickly.

Ingredients:
- 20 chicken wings, separated into 3 parts*
- 1/3 cup fermented soy sauce
- 2 inches fresh ginger, grated
- 3 cloves garlic, smashed, then chopped finely
- Juice of 1 lemon or lime
- 3 tbsp raw honey

Preheat broiler or grill on low. Mix soy sauce, ginger, garlic, juice and honey in a large, wide mixing bowl until well blended. Add wing pieces and toss to coat. If cooking under a broiler, place wings side by side on a stainless baking sheet. If cooking on a grill, place them directly on the grates. With either method, cook slowly so that the sugars in the sauce don't burn. Turn to cook second side. Pour remaining sauce in a small pot and cook down to half its volume. Baste the wings 2-3 times during cooking for a shiny, brown glaze.

* Don't discard those wing tips! **50 Ways to Eat Cock: Healthy Chicken Recipes with Balls!** will show you how to turn tips and other discarded chicken bones into an excellent and nutritious bone broth!

FINGER-LICKIN HONEY WIENERS

Serves 8

I remember having a version of this at the Hickory Farms store when we'd visit the mall as kids. It's a perfect cocktail hour treat.

Ingredients:

1 lb sausage such as kielbasa or chorizo

2-3 tbsp raw honey

Slice sausage into 1/8" rounds. Sauté over medium heat - without any additional fat - in a large skillet (sausage will render its own fat). When sausage is nicely browned all over, drizzle with honey and turn off the heat. Stir sausage until well-coated. Serve hot or cold on toothpicks.

TASTE OF HONEY PLATTER

Some of the best, most memorable dishes are the simplest. I've had variations of this in many fine restaurants and it never disappoints. Try serving this at your next big dinner party. The larger your assortment and number of guests, the larger you can make the bowl and increase the quantity of honey.

Ingredients:

- Assortment of good quality hard and semi-hard cheeses (raw milk cheeses are most flavorful) such as gruyère, brie, camembert, roquefort, pecorino romano, parmesan, stilton, cheddar, manchego etc

- Assortment of good quality deli meats such as salamis, mortadella, ham etc.

- Assortment of crispy nuts such as pecans, walnuts, and almonds

- Assortment of dried fruit such as dates, figs, unsweetened cranberries etc.

- Raw honey, preferably a clear runny type

Arrange your choices of cheeses, meats, nuts and dried fruits nicely on a platter. One or two from each category is fine. I suggest pre-slicing salamis and other deli meats as well as hard, dry cheeses like parmesan or pecorino. Prepare a small bowl with about 1/4 cup of raw honey and a spoon to place on the platter. Your guests can spoon the honey onto the cheeses, meats, nuts and fruits on their individual plates.

STICKY NUTS

Makes 4 cups

Nuts are delicious on their own, but sometimes you just want to perk them up a little. These are a sweet dessert version, but you can easily spice them up for a fiery appetizer. Note that some nuts burn faster than others, so do not mix varieties on one sheet and keep an eye on them throughout the process to make sure that you don' t end up with an expensive burned mess on your hands.

Ingredients:

4 cups crispy nuts (see Basics)

1/4 cup raw honey

1 tsp ground spices such as cinnamon, ginger and/or chili peppers (optional)

Heat oven to 325ºF. Toss nuts with honey and optional spices to coat. Lay on baking sheet. Bake for 20-30 minutes shaking the pans occasionally to prevent scorching. Remove from oven and cool.

SAUCES, SPREADS & DRESSINGS

SIZZLING CRANBERRY SAUCE

Makes one cup

Cranberry sauce has been the butt of many a joke at the Thanksgiving table. My version, suitable for any kind of poultry, pork or even lamb, will have even the pickiest eaters begging for more.

Ingredients:

   1 cup fresh or frozen whole cranberries

   1/4 cup filtered water

   1 whole 4-inch cinnamon stick

   1 inch of fresh ginger, smashed with side of a knife

   2 tbsp brandy, cognac or armagnac

   1 tbsp cold, unsalted butter

   2 tbsp raw honey

Place cranberries, water, cinnamon and ginger in a small saucepan or frying pan. Cover and cook over medium heat until cranberries have burst open. Raise heat and bring to the boil, then add brandy. Allow mixture to boil vigorously for a few minutes to burn off the alcohol. Alternately, lean back and gently tilt pan toward the flame of your stove to flambé the sauce. Once flames have died down and alcohol flavor has been cooked out, whisk in butter. Remove from heat, and then fold in honey. Serve with a smile.

HONEY BEEBEEQ SAUCE

Makes 2 cups

A version of this is used in a recipe in my other book, ***50 Ways to Eat Cock: Healthy Chicken Recipes with Balls!*** This one takes a slightly more Asian spin for a lovely result.

Ingredients:

    1 small bunch scallions, finely chopped in a food processor

    4 cloves garlic, minced

    1/2 cup tomato paste

    1/2 cup tomato purée

    1/2 cup raw cider vinegar

    1 inch fresh ginger grated

    1/2 tsp ground chili pepper

    1/4 cup raw honey

    3 tbsp toasted sesame oil

    1 Tbsp sea salt

In a covered medium-sized pot, cook first 7 ingredients over medium heat until fragrant and scallions are cooked through. Uncover and continue to cook until thick. Purée in a food processor or blender. Add honey, salt and sesame oil. Store in a glass jar in the refrigerator. Perfect for all kinds of barbecued and roasted meats — even seafood!

HONEY CASHEW BUTTER

Makes 2 cups

Cashews are a tasty treat any way you can get them. This butter is far superior to its store-bought counterparts. It makes a nice spread on toast for breakfast. *Do not prepare cashews according to the Crispy Nuts recipe in the Basics section of this book. Cashews prepared in this way will take on a foul, burnt taste.*

Ingredients:

    2 cups raw cashews

    1/4 cup extra virgin coconut oil

    1/4 cup raw honey

    1/2 tsp sea salt

Place cashews, salt and coconut oil in food processor or blender. Process on high speed until desired level of smoothness is acquired. Blend in honey. Scoop into a glass jar and store in the fridge to avoid rancidity of the cashew oil.

HONEY MUSTARD DRESSING

Makes 3/4 cup

There are two methods to making this yummy dressing. The second is a bit more foolproof and makes storage a snap. This dressing is perfect on a green salad, on a sandwich or used as a glaze on roasted meats.

Ingredients:

    2 tbsp Dijon mustard made with apple cider vinegar

    2 tbsp raw apple cider vinegar or wine vinegar

    1 small clove of garlic, smashed

    1/2 cup extra virgin olive oil

    1 tbsp raw honey

Method 1:

In a bowl, whisk together garlic, mustard and vinegar until well blended. Gradually add oil, at first only a few drops at a time, while whisking continuously. Continue whisking and adding oil to create a thick emulsion. Do not allow to "break" (oil separating from mustard mixture). Whisk in raw honey.

Method 2:

Place garlic, mustard and vinegar in a 1 cup jar with tight-fitting lid. Close with lid and shake vigorously to blend. Open lid and add about 1 tbsp of oil. Close and shake to blend. Open and add a few more tablespoons of oil. Close jar and shake. Continue until all of the oil has been added and you have a nice thick emulsion. Add honey and shake to blend.

UNDRESSED HONEY DRESSING

Makes 1/4 cup

This dressing is a bare bones version of the honey-mustard one on the previous page. I use it to dress the basic green salad that our family of 4 eats several times per week. If you grate some raw beets or carrots on your salad, it compliments the honey flavor very nicely and will win over even the pickiest eaters.

Ingredients:

>1 tbsp raw apple cider vinegar, sherry, champagne or wine vinegar

>3 tbsp extra virgin olive oil

>1 tsp raw honey

In a bowl, whisk together all ingredients. Dresses one large salad for four people.

TAKE ME NOW TOPPING

Makes 1/3 cup

This simple topping came to me when I was looking for something to perfectly accent a tropical fruit salad. Later, I realized that it is also a perfect compliment to all kinds of fruit salads, granola, nuts, and even grilled meats, where it adds a zesty tang to a plain steak as easily as it cools down a spicy sausage.

Ingredients:

> 1/4 cup whole milk, cream-line plain yogurt or sour cream
>
> 1 tbsp fresh lemon (preferably Meyer lemon) or lime juice
>
> 1 tbsp raw honey

In a bowl, mix together all the ingredients. Serve a big dollop on your favorite fruit salad or with any of the other suggestions from above.

SALADS

HONEY STRAWBERRY SALAD

Serves 4

This recipe comes from Chef Todd Mohr, founder of WebCookingClasses.com. Chef Todd's teaching style "frees people from the limitations and intimidations of the written recipe and empowers them to cook like an artist paints or a musician plays, with artistic interpretation and basic methods." Look out for this guy. He has truly started a real cooking revolution!

Ingredients:

- 1 pound strawberries, capped and sliced
- ¼ cup toasted walnuts, pecans or almonds, your pick
- ½ red onion, thinly sliced
- 2 tbsp honey
- 1 tbsp olive oil
- 2 tbsp Balsamic Vinegar
- 2 dashes Tabasco sauce
- 1/8 tsp each – salt, white pepper, cinnamon.

Combine honey, olive oil, vinegar, Tabasco, and seasonings in bowl. In a separate bowl, combine strawberries, walnuts and red onion. Lightly dress the strawberries with honey mixture. Let marinate overnight.

UNTOSSED SALAD

Serves 4

I developed this salad a few years ago while I was on vacation on the tiny Caribbean island of St. Martin, and wanted to make something a little special for dinner with my hosts. Besides only having two burners to cook on (and making dessert on one of them), the supply of fresh vegetables and good quality vinegar was scarce. This is what I came up with.

Ingredients:

    1 large onion, sliced thin lengthwise

    2 cups young red wine such as beaujolais or zinfandel

    3 fresh figs, chopped* [1]

    2 tbsp raw honey

    Sea salt, to taste

    1/4 cup extra virgin olive oil

    1 head butterhead lettuce, washed, dried and shredded

    1/2 cucumber, peeled, seeded and sliced thin

    1 small carrot, grated

    Juice of half lemon

    1 duck leg in confit, meat removed and roughly chopped

Combine onion, wine and figs in a saucepan. Simmer for half hour or more to release the natural sweetness of the onion and break down the figs. When liquid has reduced to

---

[1] If fresh are unavailable, use dried and cook longer.

1/2 cup, remove from heat. Add honey, lemon, salt and olive oil. Set aside to let cool.

In a large salad bowl, place lettuce, cucumber, and carrot. Squeeze with lemon juice and toss. Divide salad onto four plates. Top each with duck confit pieces and cooled thoroughly mixed sauce. Serve.

SOUP

WARM & FUZZY WINTER SOUP

Serves 4

If you read this book's companion, **50 Ways to Eat Cock: Healthy Chicken Recipes with Balls!**, then you know that I like to keep lots of stock on hand. It takes minimal effort to make, freezes well, and makes quick after school or work snacks. It can also the base for quick gourmet soups like this one on a hectic work night. Feel free to replace the squash with any combo of vegetables you like: mushrooms, zucchini and string beans, tomatoes and carrots, root vegetables, cauliflower etc.

Ingredients:

  2 tbsp unsalted butter

  1 medium onion, peeled and chopped

  1 stalk celery, chopped

  1 carrot, peeled and chopped

  2 delicata or 1 butternut squash, peeled, seeded and cubed

  1 bay leaf

  3 cups chicken or cock stock (from **50 Ways to Eat Cock**)

  2 cups heavy cream, preferably raw, but NOT ultra-pasteurized

  2 tbsp honey

  Celtic sea salt to taste

In a soup pot, melt butter over medium heat. Add onion, celery and carrot. Cook for 10 minutes, stirring occasionally. Next, add squash, bay leaf and stock. When all the vegetables are soft, remove the bay leaf and using a stick blender, purée the soup. Before serving, add cream, honey and salt. Continue to warm another 5 minutes. Serve immediately.

VEGETABLES

GLOSSY FRENCH TICKLED CARROTS

Serves 6

Carrots are generally considered an easy vegetable to enjoy for kids of all ages, but this recipe adds a bit of elegance to a typically mundane preparation. Slice them on a diagonal. It is not only easier to cut this way than in simple rounds, it makes a nice presentation that takes them from boring to fancy in an instant. Also, remember that carrots are already very sweet. The addition of raw honey at the finish should only enhance this sweetness, not mask it.

Ingredients:

    1 lb young carrots

    2-4 tbsp butter

    Zest of half an orange

    1 tbsp raw honey

    Sea salt, to taste

Wash and slice carrots. Cook in a few tablespoons of water and butter. When cooked through, add zest of orange and salt. Cook a bit longer to allow any excess water to boil out,

as necessary. Remove from heat and drizzle in honey. Stir to combine. Serve hot.

TANGY CUCUMBERS

Serves 4

I used to HATE cucumbers. It was probably because of the insipid flavor of non-organic ones that had been shipped across the country that I knew from my childhood. It wasn't until I joined a food co-op that gave me half a dozen cucumbers every week that I forced myself to find a recipe that even I would enjoy. This is one of them. It pairs nicely with Asian inspired dishes like Marry Me Honey Pork Chops or Chicken Teriyaki.

Ingredients:

    2 medium cucumbers, peeled, seeded and sliced thin

    1 tbsp brown rice vinegar

    1 tbsp raw honey

    Sea salt, to taste

Mix all ingredients in a bowl. Allow to marinate in the refrigerator for 30 minutes. Serve with Asian-style grilled meats or noodle dishes.

HONEY-DRIZZLED TOMATOES

Serves 4

Ingredients:

    8 plum tomatoes, sliced in half lengthwise

    2 tbsp olive oil

    Large pinch of dried Mediterranean herbs such as oregano, rosemary, basil and thyme

    Celtic sea salt, to taste

    1 tbsp raw honey

Preheat oven to 300°F. Place tomatoes cut-side up on a large baking sheet. Drizzle tomatoes with olive oil. Rubbing the herbs between your fingertips to release their flavor, sprinkle them with herbs and sea salt. Roast in oven for two hours. Drizzle on honey and continue to roast for another hour until all is soft and wilted. Serve hot or cold. These are excellent on a baguette with mozzarella or brie cheese.

HONEY-STROKED ROOT VEGETABLES

Serves 4

Most Americans these days have limited exposure to root vegetables. Roasting them is one way to make them particularly attractive to the palate. Add honey to kick them up another notch.

Ingredients:

> 4 cups assorted root vegetables such as rutabagas, turnips, beets, celeriac, carrots, parsnips, kohlrabi, sunchokes, fennel etc.
>
> 2 tbsp virgin coconut oil, lard or duck fat, melted
>
> Celtic sea salt to taste
>
> 1 tbsp raw honey

Preheat oven to 350°F. Peel and dice root vegetables into ½ inch cubes. Place on a baking pan, drizzle over fat and stir to mix. Sprinkle with salt. Bake in oven for about 20-30 minutes or until a knife can be easily inserted into the toughest vegetable (usually carrots or celeriac). When tender, drizzle with honey and stir well. Serve hot.

BREADS

CAPTIVATING CORNBREAD

Makes one 8" x 8" pan

Ingredients:

1 cup cornmeal, preferably soaked overnight in limewater**

1 cup unbleached, unenriched white flour

4 tsp baking powder

3/4 tsp Celtic sea salt

2 eggs

1 cup whole milk

1/4 cup raw honey

1/2 cup melted coconut oil, lard, bacon fat or butter

Set oven to 400°F. With all ingredients at room temperature, mix dry ingredients in one bowl. Mix wet ingredients, except fat, in a separate bowl. Add wet ingredients to dry until blended together. Drizzle fat in and mix thoroughly. Pour into a buttered and floured 8" x 8" baking dish. Bake for 20-25 minutes or until an inserted toothpick comes out clean.

° Lime water is made by soaking pickling lime or "cal" in filtered water. Pickling lime may be found in specialty, Mexican and some health food stores.

BUZZY BANANA BREAD

Makes 2 loaves

Here in Hawaii, we enjoy a large variety of exotic bananas. Often, we get so many that they are rotting before we can eat them all. This recipe is perfect for using really old, mushy bananas before they're completely unusable.

Ingredients:

2 1/2 cups unbleached, unenriched white flour

1 tsp baking powder (see Basics)

1 tsp Celtic sea salt

1 1/2 sticks unsalted butter, room temperature

1/2 cup raw honey

3 eggs, room temperature

4 large overripe bananas, smashed with the back of a fork

1 tsp dark rum

1/4 tsp freshly grated nutmeg

1/4 cup whole milk, cream line plain yogurt

1 cup chopped crispy macadamia nuts, walnuts or pecans (see Basics)

Preheat oven to 350°F. Butter a large ovenproof baking dish.

Mix together flour, baking powder, and salt in a bowl or measuring cup. Set aside.

In a large mixing bowl, blend together butter and honey until smooth and fluffy. Beat in eggs with a wooden spoon or electric mixer, one at a time until well blended. Add bananas, rum, nutmeg and sour cream. Gradually mix in flour mixture, 1/2 cup at a time. Do not over stir. Add in nuts.

Pour batter into baking dish. Bake for half an hour, or until a toothpick inserted into the middle comes out clean. Let cool. Cut into slices and serve.

SIDE DISHES

BEGUILING BAKED BEANS

Serves 6

Usually gross and kinda gummy, baked beans are usually associated with the rather rude after effect for the person eating them. With this recipe, I have never had that problem.

Ingredients:

    1/2 lb dried cannellini, navy or Great Northern beans

    Large pinch of baking soda

    1/4 lb smoked bacon, diced

    1 medium onion, cut in half

    2 cloves

    2 tbsp tomato paste

    2 tbsp blackstrap molasses

    1/4 cup raw honey

    1/4 tsp Celtic sea salt

Soak beans for at least 8 hours or overnight in a large pot of water with baking soda.*[2] After soaking, drain beans and rinse well. Place in a large pot with enough water to cover by at least an inch. Bring to the boil, then reduce heat to low. Cook for approximately 40 minutes or until tender.

Meanwhile, preheat oven to 300°F. In a flameproof casserole dish (with tight-fitting lid), sauté bacon over medium heat to

---

[2] If you haven't planned far enough ahead, boil dry beans for 5 minutes, then turn off heat, add baking soda and cover for one hour. Rinse and proceed according to rest of directions.

release the fat. Stud each half of the onion with a clove by piercing it from the outside. Add onion to fat. Cook for about 5 minutes until the onion begins to release a sweet aroma. Add beans and rest of ingredients. Stir to combine.

Add enough of the reserved water from cooking beans to cover. Cover casserole and place in oven. Bake for 3 hours. Remove cover and bake for one-half hour longer. If mixture appears to dry out at any point, add more of the reserved water, but not too much as good baked beans should have a fairly thick and syrupy sauce. Serve hot with wieners.

OOEY GOOEY YAMS

Serves 4

Most variations of candied yams are either too boring or too sickeningly sweet to enjoy. Here, they are prepared to maximize the robust, yet comforting flavor of the potatoes without overpowering them. In fact, they may remind you of sweet potato pie.

Ingredients:

1 1/2 lbs sweet potatoes, whole

2 Granny Smith apples, peeled and cut into 8 slices

3 tbsp butter

1/4 cup raw honey

1/2 tsp cinnamon

2 tbsp cognac or brandy (optional)

Pinch of Celtic sea salt

In a large pot, boil sweet potatoes in their jackets for about 20 minutes, or until cooked through. Remove potatoes from water and allow them to cool.

Meanwhile, preheat oven to 350°F. In a skillet, melt one tablespoon of butter over medium-high heat. Add apple slices and toss to cook all sides without letting them get mushy. Sprinkle with cinnamon. Raise heat and add optional cognac or brandy to pan. Boil vigorously to burn off alcohol and intensify flavor. Mix in honey and pinch of salt, and set aside.

Peel skins from potatoes and slice into rounds. Toss with apples. Dot with remaining butter and cover with aluminum foil lined with parchment. Bake for 20 minutes. Remove foil and bake another 10 minutes or until slightly crispy on top. Serve hot.

ENTREES

GLAZED HONEY CHOPS

Serves 4

These chops are delicious with a side of sauerkraut and mashed potatoes.

Ingredients:
- 4 bone-in, preferably rib portion pork chops with fat on them
- Unbleached white flour for dusting
- Ground sea salt and black pepper to taste
- Lard, coconut oil or extra virgin olive oil for light sautéeing
- 2 tbsp raw cider vinegar
- 2 tbsp raw honey

Place enough lard or oil to coat bottom of a frying pan that is large enough to hold all four chops without crowding. Heat over medium flame. Meanwhile, place some flour on a large plate. Season with salt and pepper. Dredge both sides of pork chops in flour. Cook pork chops on both sides until cooked through and nicely browned, remove to a clean plate. Turn up flame under frying pan and add vinegar. Use a spatula to scrape up any stuck pieces of flour. Turn off heat, then add honey. Stir to mix. Return chops to pan, turning to coat both sides. Serve hot.

MARRY ME HONEY CHOPS

Serves 4

Before we were married, my husband pretty much refused to eat pork, complaining that it was too dry, stringy and tough to find enjoyable. I made this recipe, allowing them to marinate for a full 4 days before cooking. Less than a week later, he requested an encore performance. Not too long after that, we got engaged. I'm pretty sure the chops had something to do with it.

Ingredients:
    4 bone-in, preferably rib portion pork chops with fat on them
    1/4 cup fermented soy sauce
    Juice of one lime
    1 clove of garlic, smashed
    2 tbsp raw honey

Mix soy sauce, lime juice, garlic and honey. Place pork chops in a ceramic dish, then pour soy mixture on top. Coat pork on both sides with sauce. Cover with plastic wrap and place in refrigerator. Turn pork chops in marinade every 8 hours or so for at least one full day. The longer you marinate, the juicier and more flavorful the final result will be. When ready to cook, place a large cast iron skillet under the broiler and heat until almost smoking. Lift pork chops out of marinade and place on hot skillet. When nicely browned on top, turn to cook second side. Total cook time should be about 15-20 minutes depending on thickness of chops and intensity of the broiler's heat. When fully cooked, move chops to a warm plate and pour marinade into skillet on the stovetop. Cook on medium heat to slightly thicken the marinade. Pour sauce over chops and serve hot.

GLISTENING BAKED HAM

Serves a whole lot of people

It's a classic that you probably haven't made totally from scratch before. This one starts by brining your own fresh ham. I actually tend to use sugar for this step because it seems too wasteful to use honey. If you do use honey for the brining, you'll probably want to use the "inferior" stuff, reserving the really great stuff for the glaze.

Ingredients:
    1 7 lb fresh ham, preferably with bone in
    1/2 lb coarse sea salt
    2 cups sugar
    1 gallon filtered water, plus 1 gallon of ice cubes
    1 tsp black or white peppercorns, crushed
    4 cloves garlic, crushed
    1/4 tsp cloves
Glaze:
    1/2 cup raw honey

In a large pot, boil salt, sugar, peppercorns, garlic and cloves in water until salt and sugar are dissolved. Cool by adding ice cubes. When water is cool enough not to actually cook the meat, add in the ham, making sure that it is completely submerged. Place a heavy plate on top to make sure it stays below the water line. Put the entire pot into the refrigerator for 3-4 days.

When ready to cook, preheat oven to 350°F. Place ham, fat-side up in a large roasting pan. Score the skin in diamond shapes to allow the fat to be released as it cooks. Cook ham for 2 hours, basting every 15 minutes. At the end of the 2 hours, baste all over with honey. Continue cooking another 30-60 minutes, basting occasionally until the internal temperature reaches 150°F. Remove from oven and allow to rest undisturbed for 15 minutes. Serve hot or cold, sliced thin, in cubes or however you want.

DRUNK & DRIPPING DUCK BREASTS

Serves 4

My good friend, Britt Malka, suggested this recipe. I made a few tweaks including replacing regular white wine with champagne and adding the honey at the last moment. This was a hit when I served it, especially with my three-year old.

Ingredients:

    4 duck breasts with skin on

    Celtic sea salt to taste

    1 four-inch cinnamon stick

    1-inch fresh ginger, grated

    1 cup champagne

    2 tbsp raw honey

In a small saucepan, heat champagne, cinnamon and ginger. Allow to boil until reduced to 1/4 cup.

Meanwhile, heat a large skillet over medium-high heat. Score skin on duck breasts in a diamond pattern without puncturing meat. Pat dry and salt lightly. Add duck breasts to hot skillet, skin-side down. Allow to brown and render most of their fat. When skin is crisp, drain most of the duck fat and reserve.* Turn duck breasts and allow to brown on second side. Cook to just below desired level of doneness (I like mine rare).

Add the strained champagne sauce to the skillet to blend with the duck juices. Baste duck with sauce and bring to rapid boil for one minute. Turn off heat. Gently mix in honey. Serve warm.

*Reserved duck fat can be used to sauté potatoes, which make a perfect accompaniment to this dish. Duck fat is also excellent for sautéing greens such as spinach or kale, or even for cooking your eggs. It's a delicious, easily digested fat.

SULTRY DUCK IN AN ORANGE DRESS

Serves 4

A classic French dish that is still an impressive crowd pleaser. Not all versions contain honey, but of course, mine does. Leftovers, if there are any, make a delicious quick lunch served with a green salad.

Ingredients:
- 2 whole ducks, poked all over with the tines of a fork
- 1/4 cup white wine, vermouth or champagne
- Juice of 2 oranges, preferably organic
- Zest of 2 oranges, preferably organic
- Sea salt to taste
- 2 tbsp raw honey

Preheat over to 300ºF. Place ducks in a large roasting pan preferably one that can be put on the stove after the initial baking. If possible, place on a rack to suspend them. This (along with poking them all over first) allows the skin to crisp and the excess fat to fall to the bottom. Season the inside of the cavity and the duck skin with salt. Grate the orange zest, then juice the orange and set aside separately. Place remaining pieces of orange inside the cavity of the duck, then place in oven to bake for 90 minutes. Duck self-bastes, so you can go do other things while it is cooking.

When meat is cooked through, move birds to a warm platter. Drain off duck fat. SAVE THIS! It is delicious in just about everything from sautéed potatoes to using to cook your eggs in for breakfast! Place the roasting pan on the stove. Deglaze the pan with wine and orange juice, scraping up any hardened bits that have collected on the bottom. Allow liquid to boil down to about half. Off heat, add zest and honey. Stir thoroughly, then return ducks to pan and *now* baste with orange sauce every 15 minutes for the next hour to form a glaze. Serve hot with potatoes sautéed in duck fat.

SILKY ASIAN CHICKEN THIGHS

Serves 4

Teriyaki is one of the easiest dishes to introduce newcomers to the delights of the Japanese table. Luckily, it's also incredibly easy to make yourself, as you will see in this recipe.

Ingredients:
- 4-6 boneless chicken thighs, skin on
- 1/4 cup fermented soy sauce
- 2 tbsp sake
- 2 tbsp mirin
- 2 tbsp raw honey

Preheat broiler with a cast iron skillet inside. Mix sauce by placing all ingredients except chicken together in a small bowl to dissolve all ingredients. Place chicken in a bowl and pour sauce over. Cover and refrigerate for at least one hour. Place chicken skin side up so that the juices and fat from the skin keep the meat moist and tender when they drip down. Turn and cook other side, basting with leftover marinade. Turn one final time and baste to give the meat a glossy coat. Meanwhile, transfer leftover marinade to a small pot and bring to the boil to cook the raw chicken juices that are in it. Serve chicken hot over rice along with the extra sauce.

MISO SALMON GLACÉ

Serves 4

Ingredients:
- 4 6-oz salmon fillets
- 2 tbsp fermented soy sauce
- 1 tbsp white or other mellow miso paste
- 2 tbsp raw honey
- 1 1-inch pice of ginger, grated

Preheat broiler or grill on low. Mix sauce by placing all ingredients except salmon together in a small pot. Warm gently to infuse flavors. Place salmon on broiler-proof baking sheet. Baste lightly with sauce. Place under broiler for 5 minutes. Flip salmon and baste the other side. Broil another 5 minutes or until done. Serve hot with remaining sauce on side.

DESSERTS

LUSCIOUS HONEY-VANILLA ICE CREAM

Makes 2 quarts

Homemade ice cream is so much yummier than store-bought. This version comes from Susan Ledbetter, who has created the popular *Honey Bee Kind* learning program in Alabama. It is completely raw, making the nutrients in the eggs, honey and cream fully available for optimal digestion and assimilation.

Ingredients:

    8 impeccably fresh raw egg yolks from pastured chickens

    2 cups full-fat raw milk, never ultra-pasteurized or homogenized

    2 cups chilled raw heavy cream, never ultra-pasteurized or homogenized

    3/4 cup raw honey

    2 tbsp vanilla extract, not imitation

Prepare your ice cream maker according to manufacturer's directions.

In a large mixing bowl, blend all ingredients until smooth being careful not to whip in any air. Start ice cream maker and slowly pour in cream mixture.

Keep ice cream maker running for approximately one half hour or until ice cream thickens. Spoon into 2 quart sized containers and freeze.

HONEY-KISSED DOUGHNUTS

Makes 2 dozen

If you want to avoid making greasy doughnuts, then you can use animal fats for frying, not vegetable oils. Animal fats are more stable for frying and result in a lighter, more digestible end result. Coconut oil is also stable, but may require you to add more oil before the batter is done.

This recipe calls for whole-wheat flour, but is just as delicious with older wheat relatives. Kamut will require slightly more liquid, while spelt and emmer will require less. Look for a firm dough in the first stage of soaking. This will ensure that the final result will not be too liquid before frying.

Ingredients:

- 2 cups whole-wheat flour (may also use spelt, kamut or emmer)
- 1 cup filtered water
- 1/4 cup yogurt or kefir
- 2 eggs
- 1 tsp baking powder
- Juice of one lemon (if desired)
- Large pinch of salt
- 3/4 cup raw honey
- One quart pastured lard, tallow or coconut

Mix flour, water and yogurt in a bowl. Cover and let stand for at least 7 hours or overnight. Add eggs, baking powder, salt, and lemon juice, if using. Stir into wheat mixture. Next, drizzle in your honey; note that it may take a few minutes to incorporate. Refrigerate mixture for 30 minutes to 2 hours.

Heat lard in a deep medium-sized saucepan over medium heat. After several minutes, hover one hand above the pot to test heat. When the heat feels as if you cannot hold your hand there for more than a few seconds without getting uncomfortable, you can test the fat by dropping a small teaspoon of batter into the pot. If the batter sizzles upon hitting the fat, then you are ready to begin frying your first batch. Spoon one full teaspoon of batter into the fat (only add one spoonful at a time). Be careful not to overcrowd the pot. Fry approximately 4 minutes on the first side before turning over to cook on the other side for another 2 minutes. Remove with a slotted spoon to drain on paper towels. Serve hot or cold.

If the test doughnut doesn't sizzle instantly, wait until this first doughnut is finished and then begin your first batch. If at any time the pot begins to smoke, reduce heat.

BEENY BROWNIES

Makes one 8" x 8" pan

A version of this recipe came to me from a friend who is repairing her digestion with a gluten-free diet. The beans used in this recipe are very easy to digest and don't require as long a soaking time as other beans such as black beans which were used in the original recipe. I actually prefer them to regular flour-based brownies because they are more satisfying and perhaps even more nutritious.

Ingredients:

>1 1/2 cups aduki beans, soaked for at least 4 hours with a pinch of baking soda
>
>1/2 cup butter, room temperature plus more for greasing pan
>
>6 tbsp cocoa
>
>2 tbsp blackstrap molasses
>
>1/2 cup raw honey
>
>1/4 tsp sea salt
>
>4 eggs lightly beaten

Boil aduki beans in fresh filtered water until soft, approximately 30-40 minutes. Preheat oven to 350°F. In a food processor, process beans to a smooth paste. Try not to add too much of the water that they have boiled in or it will make the final product difficult to hold together. Add rest of the ingredients and mix until well-blended. Grease an 8 x 8-inch baking pan with some butter. Pour in batter. Bake in oven for 45-50 minutes until a toothpick inserted in the center comes out clean. Allow to cool. Cut into small squares for a rich and tasty after dinner treat.

RICOTTA WITH HONEY DRIZZLES

Serves 2

This is a lovely recipe that comes from the Italian tradition. I'm lucky to get ricotta direct from a local farm, so I always make sure keep some on hand for the midnight crazies.

Ingredients:

   1 cup whole milk ricotta cheese

   1/4 cup crispy walnuts, crushed by hand (see Basics)

   2 tbsp raw honey, preferably from flowers such as lavender or orange blossom

Spoon ricotta into 2 dessert bowls. Sprinkle with walnuts. Gently warm honey in small saucepan over low heat -- just enough to liquify it, if it's too thick and creamy to pour. Drizzle over cheese and nuts. Enjoy!

BLAZING APPLE DELIGHT

Serves 4

I make a killer apple pie, but don't take the time to do it most of the year. This alternative to baking a full pie takes about 10 minutes from start to finish and is a favorite in our house. In fact, when we eat this, we don't miss the crust at all!

Ingredients:

    2 tbsp unsalted butter

    3 large tart, firm apples such as Granny Smith, Rome or Gala

    1 tbsp liquor such as armagnac, cognac or brandy (optional)

    Dash cinnamon

    Freshly grated nutmeg

    1 tsp raw honey

    Whipped Cream of the Gods (next page)

Peel, core and slice apples into 8-12 slices each. Melt butter in a large heavy bottomed skillet over high heat. Add apples and toss to coat. You want the apples to brown slightly and caramelize on the outside, not to turn to mush. Add liquor, if using. Lean your head back and tilt pan toward flame to allow liquor to catch the flame, which burns off the alcohol. When flame dies down, add cinnamon, nutmeg and drizzle in honey. Toss to coat. Serve hot with cool whipped cream.

WHIPPED CREAM OF THE GODS

Serves 4

Instead of a whisk, sometimes I just shake the cream in a mason jar or old mayonnaise jar. Makes storage super-simple.

Ingredients:

    1 cup heavy cream, cold and preferably raw

    1 tsp real vanilla extract in alcohol or glycerin

    2 tsp raw honey

Place cream in a bowl, whisk until thick, being careful not to turn it into butter. Gently whisk in vanilla. Whisk in honey, one teaspoon at a time. Good on just about anything!

ALEX'S PEACHES ITALIANO

Serves 4

Larry Broderick, Regional Account Director at Extended Stay Hotels (my personal favorite lodging choice), is a HUGE fan of peaches. So when I asked him to contribute a honey recipe, he chose this one named for his son. You can learn more about Larry and his love of great food at: www.linkedin.com/in/larrybroderickesh.

Ingredients:

　　2 almost ripe peaches, halved and stones removed

　　2 tbsp gorgonzola cheese

　　Balsamic vinegar, for drizzling

　　Blueberry-infused raw honey*

Grill peaches flesh side down for about 5 minutes over medium heat. Flip them. After two minutes add a grape size piece of gorgonzola cheese to the middle of each peach half. As the cheese JUST starts to melt, remove it from heat. Drizzle with balsamic vinegar and blueberry infused raw honey.

* Larry sources this honey from a local beekeeper, who mixes blueberry syrup into his honey. If this is unavailable where you live, feel free to use plain raw honey or another flavor that you can get in your neck of the woods.

HONEY BLUEBERRY CRUMBLE

Makes one 9" deep-dish pie

Years ago, I had planned to bake pecan cookies for a get together at a friend's house. The cookies wouldn't hold together. Luckily, I had a bag of organic blueberries in the freezer and this recipe was born. I start the crust the day before by soaking the nuts and oats to unlock maximum nutrition.

Ingredients:

    16 oz fresh or frozen organic blueberries

    1/4 cup + 2 tbsp raw honey

    Juice of half lemon

    2 tbsp arrowroot starch

    1/2 cup rolled oats

    1/4 cup whole milk, cream line plain yogurt

    2 cups filtered water

    1 cup crispy pecans (see Basics)

    1/2 tsp Celtic sea salt + a pinch

    1 tbsp butter

In a bowl, mix oats with yogurt. If too thick to coat oats, add some filtered water until oats are all coated, but not swimming in yogurt. Cover and set aside. In a separate bowl, place pecans with a 1/2 tsp of salt and filtered water. Cover and set aside. Both bowls should sit at room temperature for 7-8 hours.

Preheat oven to 350ºF. In a bowl, mix blueberries, 1/4 cup of honey, lemon juice, starch and a pinch of salt. Pour into your pie dish. Place on center rack in oven.

Drain pecans thoroughly. Place in mortar and pestle and roughly crack them, or place on cutting board and roll over them with a rolling pin. Mix with oats and remaining two tablespoons of honey. Sprinkle the entire mixture over blueberries. Dot with butter. Return to oven and bake for 20 minutes or until golden brown on top and blueberries are bubbling. Serve warm.

HONEY-POACHED PEARS

Serves 6

Poached fruit is an elegant, sensual dessert that is often overlooked in today's gooey, multi-layer, molten lava, frosted fudge cake world. It is great just on its own, but also pairs (see what I did there?) nicely with a dollop of whipped cream. If you don't have pears on hand, you can substitute apples, peaches or apricots.

Ingredients:

6 firm pears, preferably Bosc, peeled, cored and quartered

1 quart filtered water

1/3 cup raw honey

1 cinnamon stick

Zest of one lemon, peeled of in large pieces that can be removed later

Place water, honey, cinnamon and lemon zest in a pot. Bring to the boil, then reduce heat to low. Gently place pears into water and simmer for 20 minutes. Let cool. Remove cinnamon and zest. Serve pears lukewarm or cold in bowls with their liquid.

BODACIOUS BAKLAVA

Serves 4

No book of honey recipes would be complete without a recipe for baklava. Oh, and by the way, you can't just make a little baklava. It is always made in a huge, family-sized pan. You know, the one you use for lasagna. That said, the serving size in the Middle East and eastern Mediterranean countries where this dessert is common is about 1/4 of what they serve in the U.S.

Ingredients:

15 sheets of 17" x 12" phyllo dough, thawed in refrigerator, if frozen

1/2 lb unsalted butter or ghee, melted and cooled

3 cups crispy pistachios or walnuts, roughly chopped by hand (see Basics)

1/2 cup filtered water

1 cup raw honey

1 tbsp fresh lemon juice

Unroll phyllo. Using a sharp knife, cut sheets in half so that they are now 12" x 8-1/2". Stack on top of one another and keep covered with a kitchen towel so they don't dry out.

Preheat oven to 350ºF. Butter a 9" x 13" baking dish. Place one sheet of at bottom of baking dish. Brush on melted butter and place another sheet over top being careful not to get the butter solids onto them because they will burn when baked. Repeat this process until you have 10 sheets stacked with butter in between each sheet. Brush butter on top sheet, then sprinkle with half of the nuts. Continue layering phyllo and butter for another 10 sheets. After buttering top sheet, sprinkle with remaining nuts. Then repeat layering phyllo and butter until all sheets are used up.

Cut into traditional diamond shape by slicing lengthwise into long strips at 1-3/4" intervals, then cutting on a diagonal at 1 1/2" apart from one another. Brush on remaining butter, making sure the entire top is buttered. Bake for 50 minutes until golden.

Meanwhile, mix water, honey and lemon juice in a saucepan. Bring to the boil, then reduce liquid slightly until mixture is syrupy, about 5 minutes.

Remove baklava from oven and let cool for 10 minutes. Pour syrup over top. Let cool thoroughly at room temperature for at least 12 hours so that all the layers can soak up the syrup. Serve at room temperature.

Baklava can be stored at room temperature for up to 5 days.

SWEET REMEDIES

KRUPNIKAS

Alcohol in a health cookbook? You bet! While I don't necessarily recommend drinking distilled alcohol on a daily basis, many societies enjoy small amounts often as a digestive aid or cold remedy. In Lithuania, *krupnikas* is traditionally used for the latter. Note that it is completely normal for *krupnikas* to be cloudy. Simply shake the bottle before serving to mix in all of the spices. Alternately, you can just pour off the clear liquid leaving the sediment at the bottom of the bottle. Either way, it is warming and delicious.

Ingredients:

2 lbs clover honey

1 qt. of grain alcohol such as Everclear, however, a lower proof alcohol is fine

2 qts. water

10 whole cloves

10 cardamom pods

1 tbsp caraway seeds

1 vanilla bean split

3 cinnamon sticks, broken in half or thirds

½ nutmeg seed

4 pieces of peeled fresh ginger the size of your thumb, cut into smaller pieces

2 or 3 pieces of orange peel, try not to get the white pith when slicing

2 or 3 pieces of lemon peel, same

pinch of saffron strands

With a mortar and pestle crack the cloves, cardamom and nutmeg (don't crush very much). Break the cinnamon sticks in half. Add all spices into the water and boil until water reduced by half. Bring honey to a boil and spoon off the foam. Add the spice water to the honey.

Remove honey spice water from stove and away from any flames, slowly add grain alcohol. Filter *krupnikas* through a coffee filter into a clean and sanitized large lidded jar. Place in a cool, dark place for at least 3 weeks, then pour into clean sanitized bottles with rubber stoppers, such as Grolsch beer bottles.

Serve at room temperature or warm gently in a pot on the stove.

NAUGHTY HOT TODDY

Serves 1

Hot toddies were frequently prescribed years ago for fevers accompanied by sore throats and general conditions of malaise. They have largely fallen out of favor to make way for patented pharmaceuticals. Even so, some people still drink them on a cold winter day because they warm you up, relax you and taste so damn good!

Ingredients:

    1 ounce good quality dark rum or whisky

    1 tbsp fresh lemon juice

    1 tbsp raw honey

    1 cup freshly boiled water

Combine all ingredients. Stir. Sip slowly when water has cooled enough for you.

SLIPPERY SORE THROAT SOOTHER

Makes 1/4 cup

I've seen many variations of this simple remedy, which is useful for both sore throats and coughs. Thus far, I haven't found any varieties to be more effective than this one. Note that if you don't double dip the spoon with your cooties, you can use leftovers to make many of the other recipes in this book.

Ingredients:

    2 tbsp fresh-squeezed lemon juice

    2 tbsp raw honey

Mix both ingredients together. Take one teaspoon occasionally allowing the syrup to trickle down your throat to relieve the soreness and/or coughing fits.

HIGH ENERGY DRINK

Makes 1 quart

My friend, Lisa Richards, is great at making her own versions of commercially available and often expensive foods. Here's her answer to one of Bragg's apple cider vinegar beverages reputed to increase your energy without caffeine.

Ingredients:

    1 tbsp apple cider vinegar

    1-2 tbsp raw honey

    Juice of one half lemon (or a whole lemon, if not juicy enough)

    Pinch of cinnamon

    Pinch of Celtic sea salt

    4 cups filtered water

Mix all ingredients in a quart-sized container, mason jar or recycled glass juice bottle. Serve chilled.

TITILLATING HONEY TURNIP

Here's a natural cough remedy that comes to me from my good friend and farmer, Smadar, of Genesis Farm in northwest New Jersey. I haven't needed it myself, but she swears by the turnip's effectiveness in stopping coughs and related disorders like hoarseness, sore throat and congestion.

Ingredients:

   1 whole turnip, preferably black

   Raw honey

Wash turnip of all dirt and cut off the bottom so that it can rest on a flat surface. Cut off top of turnip and hollow out the turnip by inserting a paring knife and cutting a circle on an angle. Do not cut clear through to the bottom. You want the turnip to be like a small bowl to be able to hold a few teaspoons of the honey. Fill the hole of the turnip with honey. Place in a bowl and cover with a plate or piece of plastic wrap. Let sit for 2-3 hours until honey has passed through the turnip. You will have a very watery and fairly clear liquid collected in the bowl.*[3] Drink this liquid. You can repeat the process at least 3 more times with the same turnip to get its cough-stifling benefits.

---

   [3] Sometimes the honey doesn't pass through the turnip. You will know its ready, though, because it will simply turn liquid instead of remaining in its stickier state.

SWEET & SPICY CURE-ALL

Many people believe that the combination of honey and cinnamon will cure just about anything. This dynamic duo has been reported to offer relief from bladder infections, arthritis, gas, flu, pimples, skin infections, fatigue, bad breath, and even obesity and cancer. Here's the basic recipe that should be taken before breakfast and again at bedtime. Specific conditions may require small adjustments in doses and frequency. *PLEASE consult your doctor before using this protocol, especially for sugar sensitive individuals such as hypoglycemics and diabetics.*

Ingredients:

    1 tsp raw honey

    1/2 tsp cinnamon powder

    1 cup freshly boiled water

Mix all ingredients. Serve hot.

BEE STING ALLERGY OBLITERATOR

Allergies are the scourge of the modern world. I have long known people to use this "recipe" for seasonal allergies such as hay fever, but more recently my friend, Andrea Schmitz, told me that she cured four of her six children of bee sting allergies this way! *PLEASE consult your doctor before trying this one.*

Ingredient:

> Raw local honey from bees within 50 miles of where you live

That's it! Just consume a few teaspoons per day, throughout the day, during allergy season.

BASICS

BAKING POWDER

I haven't bought baking powder in over 15 years. It's so simple and inexpensive to make yourself, there's no reason not to.

Ingredients:

    4 tbsp arrowroot starch

    4 tbsp cream of tartar

    2 tbsp baking soda

Mix all ingredients together. Store in a tightly closed jar.

CRISPY NUTS

This recipe comes from my go-to cookbook for all things healthy, *Nourishing Traditions*, by Sally Fallon and Dr. Mary Enig. Soaking and drying nuts as described in the book helps them to retain most of their enzymes and nutrients, while making them easy on the digestive tract. My family always has plenty of these on hand, especially for road trips.

Ingredients:

    4 cups walnuts, pecans, almonds or macadamia nuts

    1 tbsp Celtic sea salt

    Filtered water

In a large bowl, sprinkle nuts with sea salt and cover with filtered water. Cover with a plate. Soak for seven hours or overnight at room temperature. Drain nuts and place on a lined baking sheet. Bake nuts in a low oven between 125° and 140°F tossing occasionally several hours until thoroughly dried. Cool completely before storing in glass jars.

APPENDIX

MEASUREMENTS & EQUIVALENTS

a dash = 8 drops (liquid) ≈ ⅛ teaspoon (slightly less)

1 tsp = 1 teaspoon = 60 drops
3 tsp = 3 teaspoons = 1 tablespoon = ½ fluid ounce

½ T = ½ tablespoon = 1½ teaspoons
2 T = 2 tablespoons (liquid) = 1 fluid ounce = ⅛ cup
3 T = 3 tablespoons = 1 ½ fluid ounces = 1 jigger
4 T = 4 tablespoons = ¼ cup

⅛ C = ⅛ cup = 2 tablespoons
⅙ C = ⅙ cup = 2 tablespoons + 2 teaspoons
⅓ C = ⅓ cup = 5 tablespoons + 1 teaspoon
1 C = 1 cup = ½ pint = 8 fluid ounces
2 C = 2 cups = 1 pint = 16 fluid ounces
4 C = 4 cups = 1 quart = 2 pints = 32 fluid ounces
4 quarts = 1 gallon

1 peck = 8 quarts = 2 gallons
1 bushel = 4 pecks

RESOURCES

Bees, Beekeeping and Honey: Early Honey History, Healthmont Honey, Australia, 2012.

Bock, Linda, State Doesn't Know if Listeriosis Outbreak is Over, News Telegram, January 2008.

Brownstein, David, Salt Your Way to Health, Medical Alternative Press, 2006.

Byrnes, Stephen, Diet & Heart Disease: It's NOT What You Think..., Whitman Publications, 2001.

Enig, Mary, Know Your Fats: The Complete Primer for Understanding the Nutrition of Fats, Oils, and Cholesterol, Bethesda Press, 2000.

Enig, Mary and Fallon, S., Nourishing Traditions: The Cookbook that Challenges Politically Correct Nutrition and the Diet Dictocrats, Hudson Street Press, 1995.

Enig, Mary and Fallon, S., Oiling of America, The Weston A. Price Foundation, January 1, 2000.

Engeseth, N. J., Wang, X., and Gheldof, N., Buckwheat Honey Increases Serum Antioxidant Capacity in Humans, Journal of Agricultural and Food Chemistry, 51(5), 1500-1505, 2003.

Erskine, James, Langworthy, George et al., Vanishing Of The Bees, The Co-operative Group, 2009.

Fleming, D.W., S.L. Cochi, et al., Pasteurized Milk as a Vehicle of Infection in an Outbreak of Listeriosis, The New England Journal of Medicine, Volume 312:404-407, February 14, 1985.

HoneyAssociation.com, A Brief History of Honey, n.d., Web. 20 Jul. 2014.

Hoppenhaus Kerstin and Imhoof Markus, More Than Honey, Zero One Film, 2012.

Horn, T., Honey Bees: A History, The New York Times, April 11, 2008.

Lau, C. W., Ancient Chinese Apiculture, Bee World, December 2012.

Lu, Henry C., Chinese Natural Cures: Traditional Methods for Remedies and Preventions, Black Dog & Leventhal Publishers, Inc., 1994.

Pizzorno, Joseph E. and Michael T. Murray, Textbook of Natural Medicine, Churchill Livingstone, 2000.

Pritchford, Paul, Healing with Whole Foods: Oriental Traditions and Modern Traditions, North Atlantic Books, 1993.

Molga, P., La mort des abeilles met la planète en danger, Les Echos, August 20, 2007

Monastyrsky, Konstantin, <u>Fiber Menace: The Truth About the Leading Role of Fiber in Diet Failure, Constipation, Hemorrhoids, Irritable Bowel Syndrome, Ulcerative Colitis, Crohn's Disease, and Colon Cancer</u>, Ageless Press, 2005.

Omovalley.com, <u>Bodi or Me'en Tribe In Omo Valley in Ethopia</u>, n.d., Web. 20 Jul. 2014.

Paetzke, D, <u>The Story of Honey,</u> National Honey Board, n.d., Web. 20 Jul. 2014.

Rabbi, B., <u>Apples and Honey</u>, Aish.com., September 24, 2005.

Roddy, K. M., and Arita-Tsutsumi, L., <u>A History of Honey Bees in the Hawaiian Island,</u> J. Hawaiian Pacific Agriculture., 8, 59-70., 1997.

Ryan, C.A., M.K. Nickels et al., <u>Massive Outbreak of Antimicrobial-Resistant Salmonellosis Traced to Pasteurized Milk</u>, The Journal of the American Medical Association, Vol. 258 No. 22, December 11, 1987.

Sahba, A., <u>The mysterious deaths of the honeybees</u>, CNN Money, March 29, 2003.

Schramm, D. D., <u>Honey with High Levels of Antioxidants Can Provide Protection to Healthy Human Subjects</u>. *Journal of Agricultural and Food Chemistry*, 51(6), *1732*-1735, 2003.

Siegel, T., Queen of the Sun, Collective Eye Films, 2010. DVD.

Vonderplanitz, Aajonus, We Want to Live, Carnelian Bay Castle Press, LLC, 1997.

Whitney, E.N. and S.R. Rolfes, Understanding Nutrition, Ninth Edition, Wadsworth Group, 2002.

Williams, David G., Conquering Arthritis Through Natural Methods, Mountain Home Publishing, 1994.

A SPECIAL GIFT FOR YOU!

Fifty Honey recipes not enough? I had to cut this book off at 50 recipes to keep it with the Affordable Organics & GMO-Free Series, but I have some special bonus recipes that I wanted to share with you. Now you can get your hands on these exclusive recipes just for purchasing this book.

The recipes in this gift are donated by some of my favorite honey producers and body care professionals. I'm sure you're going to love them.

Go to http://honeyling.us/bonus to claim your free gift today!

ABOUT THE AUTHOR

Adrienne Hew has been called "the Nutrition Heretic" and "the Pope of Health" because she challenges the sacred cows of cult-like diets. Her unique insight has both Dietetic Associations and politically correct, so-called alternative health advocates scrambling to justify their broken theories about health that have contributed to the current outbreak of new and seemingly irreparable diseases.

Ms. Hew began her holistic health journey after suffering innumerable health problems while following the American Dietetics Association's dietary recommendations. Her brush with death, after being treated by a now very popular vegan doctor, set her on a quest to learn the dietary commonalities amongst all healthy societies. Using her fluency in three languages, she has been able to uncover many long forgotten food traditions throughout the world.

Receiving a certificate in Chinese dietetics in 2002 and her degree as a Certified Nutritionist in 2004, she has helped many clients and workshop attendees to decode their own health dilemmas by understanding the inconsistencies in conventional nutritional dogma. As a cook, her recipes have been popular with everyone from celebrated chefs to picky 4 year olds and adults who "don't eat that". She currently resides in Hawaii with her husband and two children.

She can be found online at http://www.nutritionheretic.com as well as on her Facebook fan page (http://www.facebook.com/TheNutritionHeretic) and on Twitter (http://twitter.com/NutriHeretic).

Printed in Great Britain
by Amazon.co.uk, Ltd.,
Marston Gate.